Harbours of Ireland

Dedicated to the memory of my father, Rod O'Shea whose support ensured that I followed my path as an artist.

This edition published 1995 by
John Hinde Limited, Dublin 18, Ireland.
under licence from The Ugly Duckling Co. Limited.

Edited by Donald Sutherland and Róisín O'Shea.

Acknowledgments:
Caitriona Foley and Marie Mulligan,
research assistants.

An Artists Portfolio

Harbours of Ireland

A Collection of Pen & Ink & Watercolour paintings by Irish artist Róisín O'Shea.

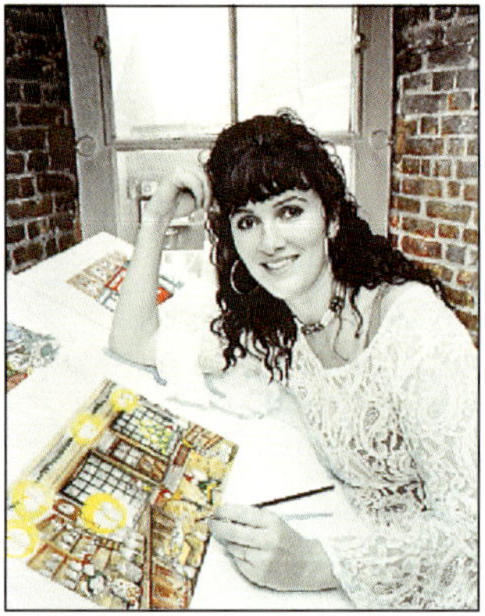

Born in Cork, Ireland in 1960, Róisín O'Shea studied at the National College of Art and Design, Dublin, and following graduation headed to Sydney, Australia, where she completed a post-graduate diploma in the City Art Institute. On her return in 1985 she continued painting, drawing her inspiration from her native landscape which continues to captivate her today. In her 19 years of painting Róisín has built up an enormous collection of sketches, paintings and photographs from the length and breadth of Ireland which led to this series of books.

INTRODUCTION

Circumnavigation of Ireland taking the shortest route is a journey of about 1,200kms. This of course is avoiding all the coastal inlets. Ireland's true coastline, inlets included, measures a little over 3,200kms and, due to its island status, holds nearly forty percent of the European Union's fishing waters – an estimated 208,000 square kms of sea. The island of Ireland comprises thirty-two counties, of which half do not have sea harbours. The remaining sixteen counties have a total of fifty commercial and fishing harbours representing some of the most breathtaking scenes found in Ireland. As an island we were extremely vulnerable to invasion; the Spaniards, for example, unsuccessfully attempted to invade Ireland on two different occasions, both of which ended in disaster. In 1588 an Armada of over 140 Spanish ships sailed to Ireland's west coast. Stretching from County Donegal to County Clare, it is estimated that well over fifty ships struggled against the strong Atlantic coast, crashing against the rugged rocky coastline in a series of severe gale force winter storms. Those sailors that survived the initial storms made their way to shore, only to be murdered as they staggered out of the rough surf. A few of the Armada ships managed to keep going, some being forced to stop in Kinsale in County Cork and others going as far as Dungarvan, County Waterford. Those fortunate sailors were taken in by the local people, given lots of local brew and home-cooked meals, and soon settled in their respective towns. So far, seventeen wrecks from that Armada have been located along the west coast of Ireland and traces of the Spanish influence can still be found in quite a few of the west and south-west coastal towns and villages. The subject matter of this volume deals with my personal selection of harbours of Ireland, excluding island harbours which will be covered in another volume.

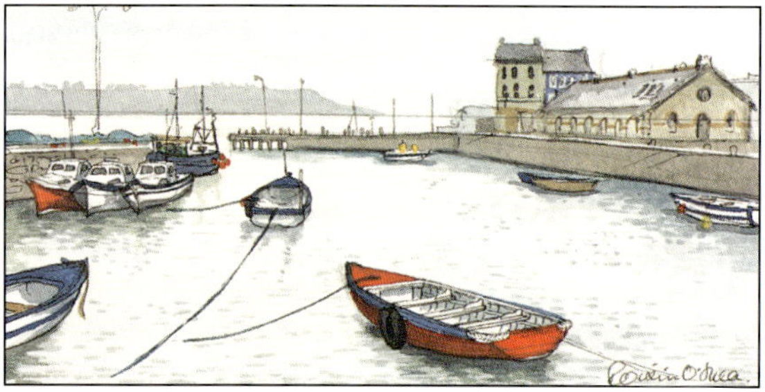

YOUGHAL, CORK

This harbour is situated near the River Blackwater estuary and opens into Youghal Bay. Already a sprawling village in the 1400s, Youghal was invaded by Roger Mortimer on Easter Sunday 1317. He intended to challenge the Bruces and their allies who had settled in the region. Youghal is now a well-known resort town with a wealth of good pubs and restaurants.

KINSALE, CORK

This is a natural harbour formed by the estuary of the Bandon River. The Lusitania was torpedoed off the Old Head of Kinsale on 7th May 1915, with the loss of 1,198 lives. It was a determining factor in the U.S.A. joining forces with the Allies against Germany. In 1601 some of the Spanish Armada landed at Kinsale. The Spanish fleet consisted of 3,000 men; reduced by adversity from a force of 6,000, they were far too weak to withstand the subsequent blockade of the harbour by the Anglo-Irish Privy council. Irish chieftains O'Neill and O'Donnell decided to lend what strength they could to the Spanish. The ensuing battles led to many Irish being killed. The town of Kinsale is now known for its hospitality and international cuisine.

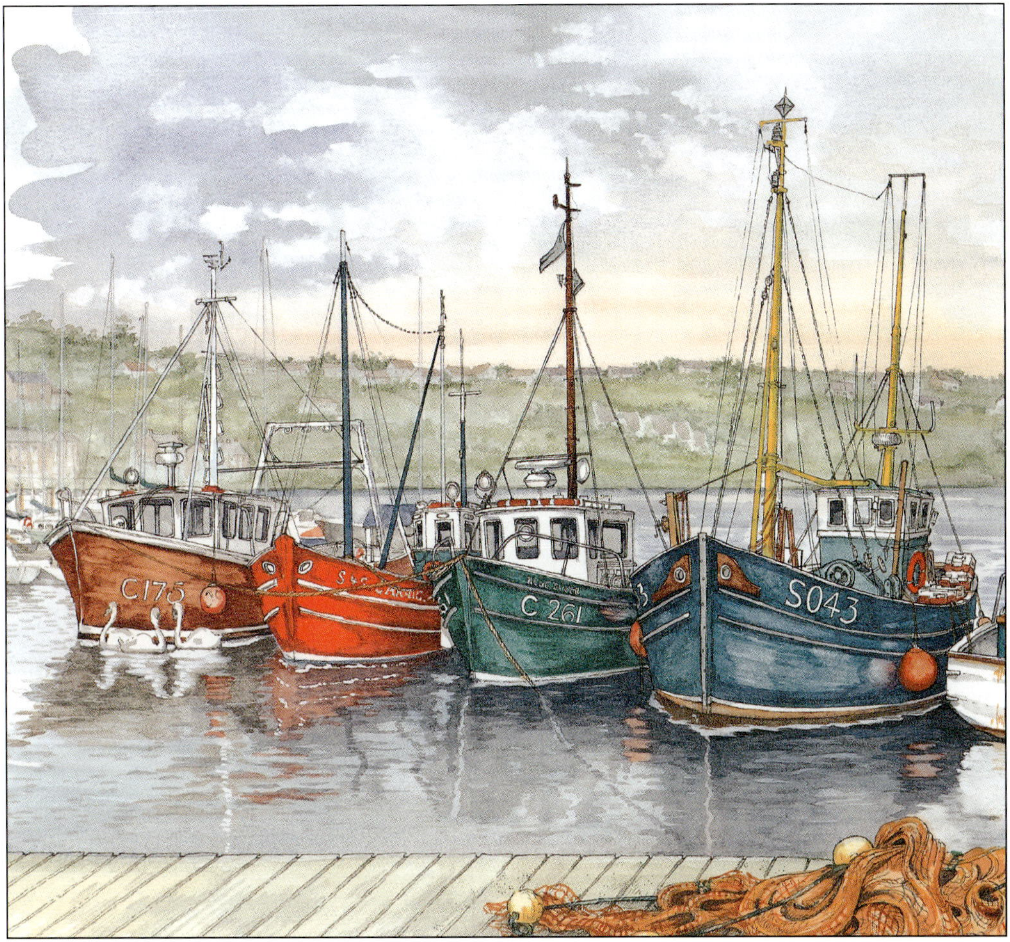
C175
C 261
S043

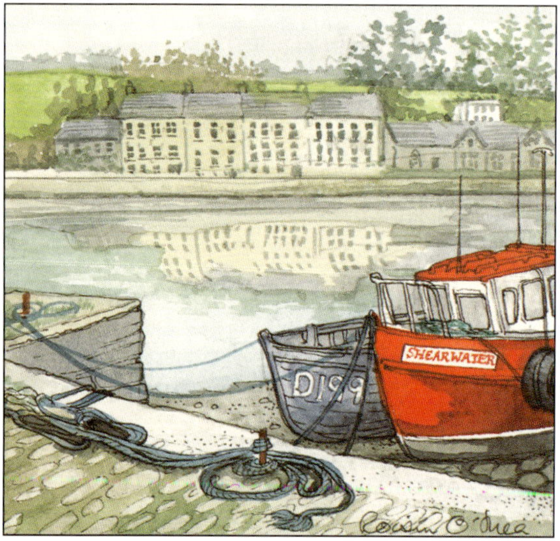

BANTRY, CORK

Bantry Harbour is mostly concerned with commercial activity, but there are some yachts for hire. Bantry's harbour is large enough to accommodate a number of coasting vessels, along with anchorage for one-quarter ton tankers. In 1689 and 1796 there were two failed invasion attempts by the French.

COBH, CORK

Emigrants left Ireland from three harbours – Londonderry or Derry, Dublin (usually to Liverpool and then to the Americas), and the most popular Cobh (pronounced Cove). Cobh harbour is steeped in nautical history and should you get the opportunity, I highly recommend visiting the historical centre there. Cobh was the harbour for the first transatlantic steamship crossing to the Americas in 1838 as well as the last port of call on the ill-fated maiden voyage of one of the greatest luxury liners of the twentieth century, the Titanic. The emigration trail that took place in the 1800s was the greatest tragedy for the Irish. In 1852 over 300,000 Irish emigrated to the Americas in what became known as coffin ships because of severe overcrowding.

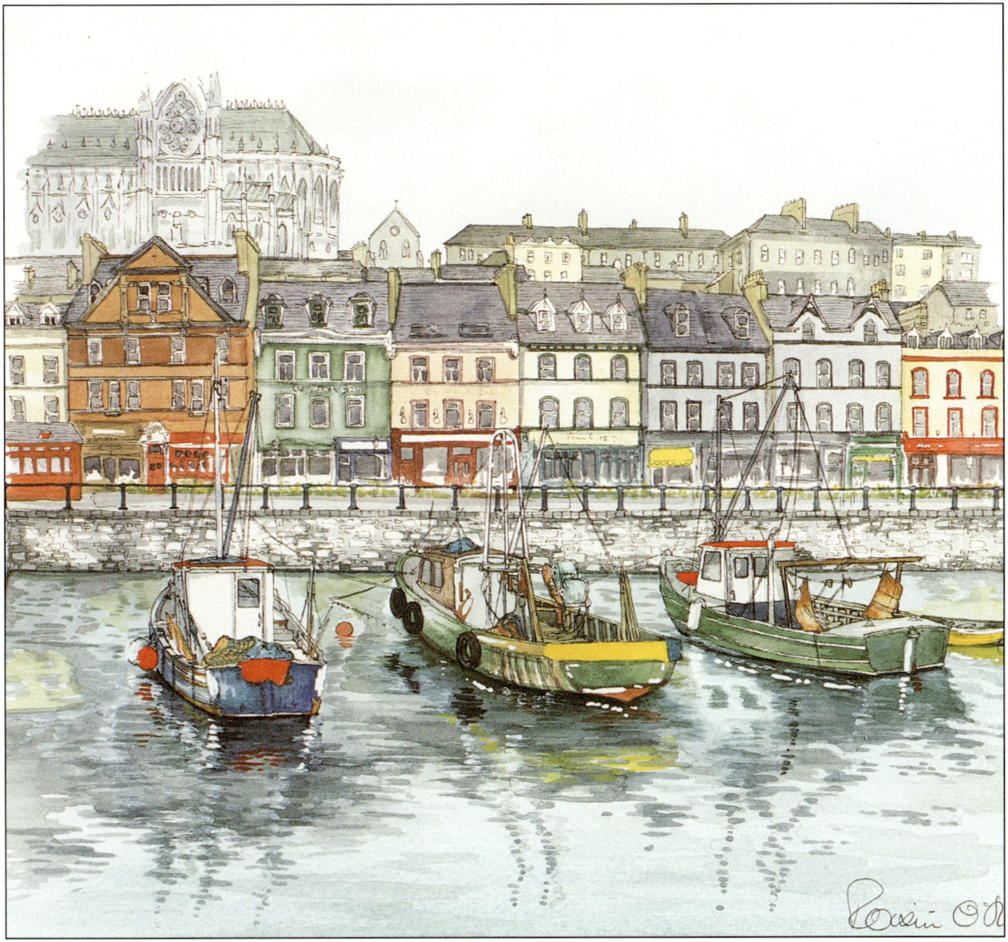

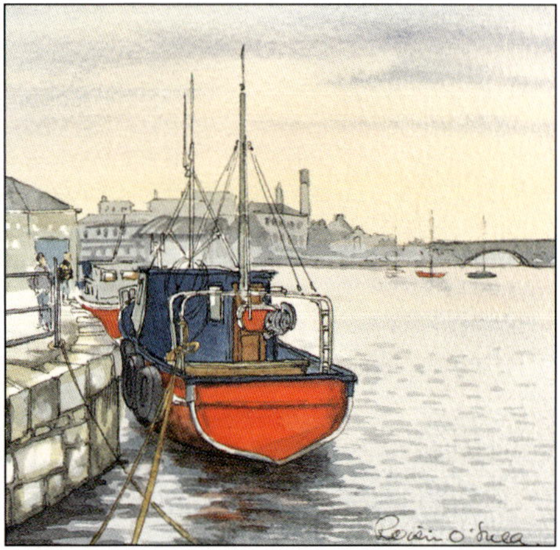

DUNGARVAN, WATERFORD

A town in which I spent much of my summer childhood, Dungarvan holds many fond memories for me – the annual horse-show, chips and sausages from Willie's and Paddy's (who have since retired), the ritual Sunday lunch in Lawlor's hotel where without fail I would have a chocolate sundae for dessert. For my father it was the occasional trip from the harbour to go shark fishing. In the intervening years Dungarvan has remained relatively unchanged and still offers that 'time-out' atmosphere, a welcome change from the fast pace of urban living.

HELVICK HEAD, WATERFORD

A beautifully tranquil and picturesque harbour, Helvick Head is a few minutes' drive from Dungarvan. My father took us boating across the bay on many occasions, and it still has that special magic of a place that time forgot.

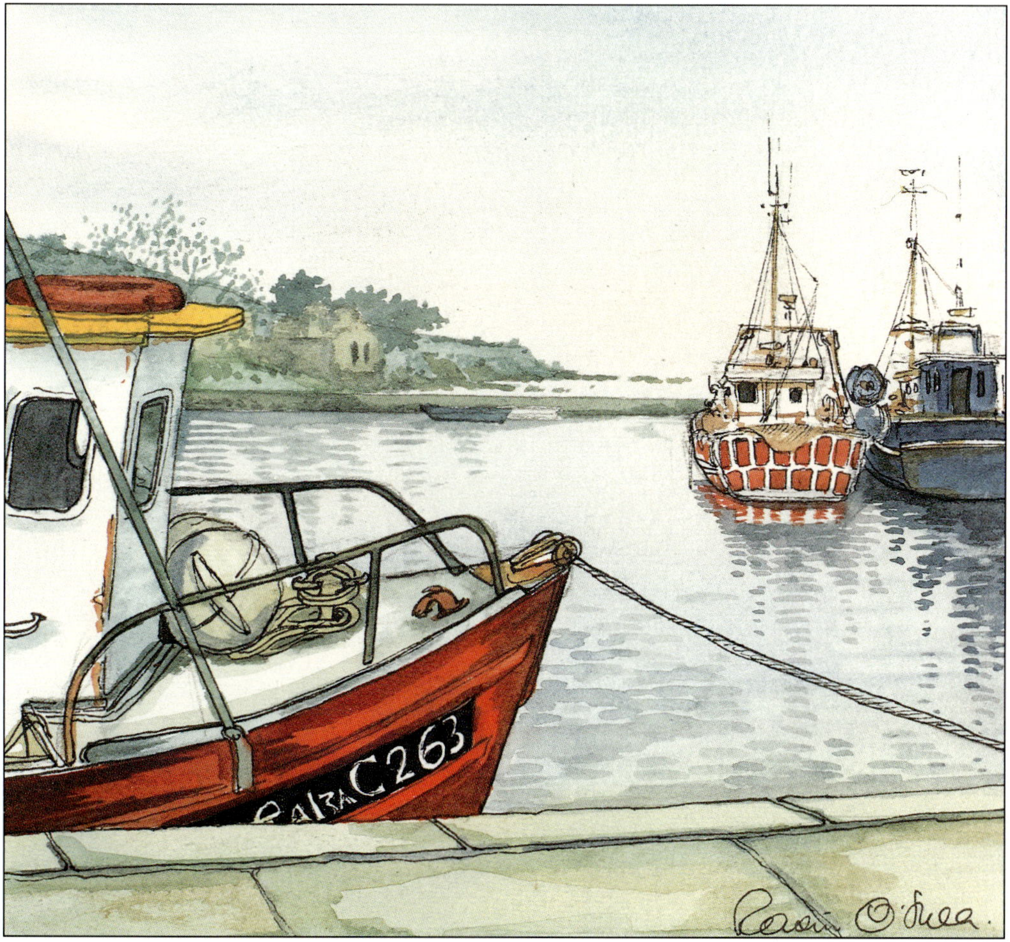
C263

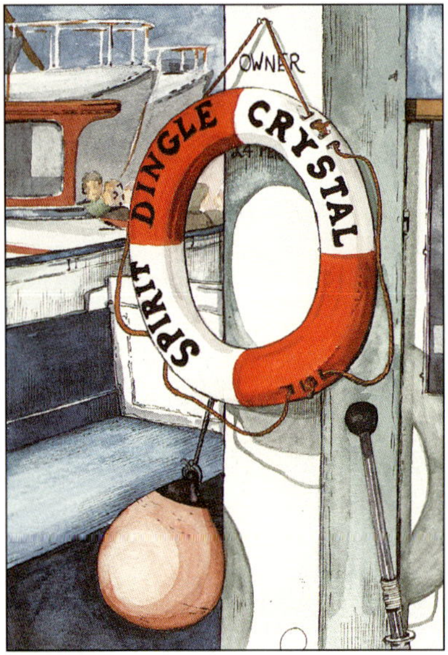

LIFE BELT, KERRY

For those who would like a close view of Funghi the dolphin there are boats that take visitors out into the harbour. This painting is a detail from the boat that took me on my last trip.

DINGLE, KERRY

Funghi the Dingle dolphin is perhaps the best known bottle-nosed dolphin in Irish waters. This type of dolphin is very common around Ireland. The Latin name is Tursiops truncatus, is thought to be very intelligent and can relate somewhat with humans. Dolphins are renowned for their therapeutic powers – people with various mental and physical disabilities will often swim with them and have been known to experience some relief. I was exhilarated by my own experience swimming with Funghi, though I would recommend wearing a wet-suit as I barely survived the cold waters; for revival, a pint of Guinness in Dick Mac's pub is essential.

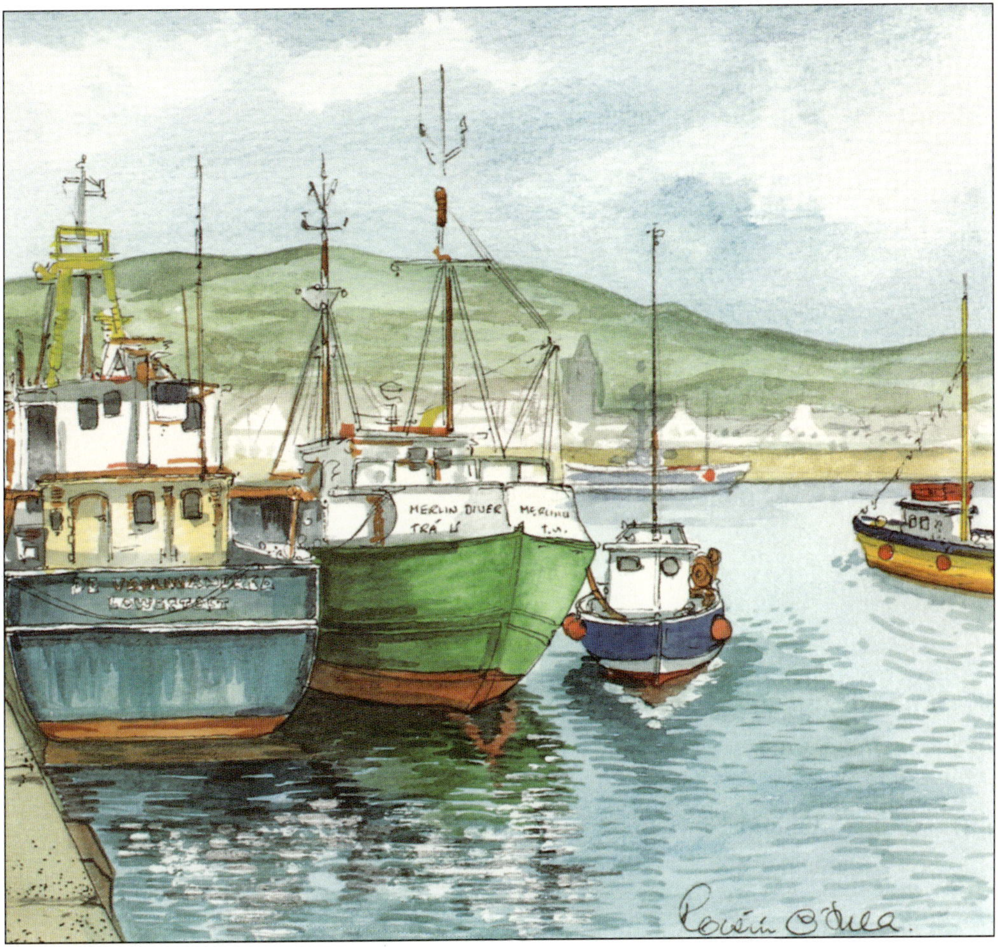
MERLIN DIVER

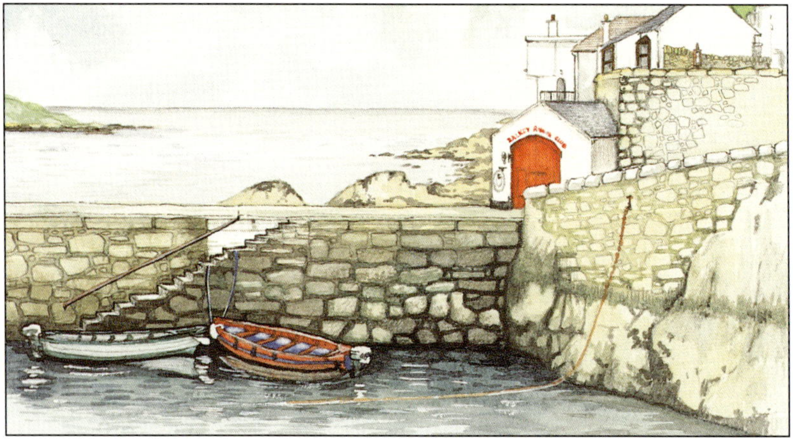

BOATSHED, COLIEMORE, DUBLIN

COLIEMORE, DUBLIN

From Coliemore Harbour one can see Dalkey Island with its famous Martello Tower. The Irish for Dalkey is Delginis, which means Thorn Island. The Danes, who had a fortress here in the 10th century, gave Dalkey its present name. Delg was changed into 'Dalk' – the Danish for thorn, and Inis into 'ey' – Danish for island.

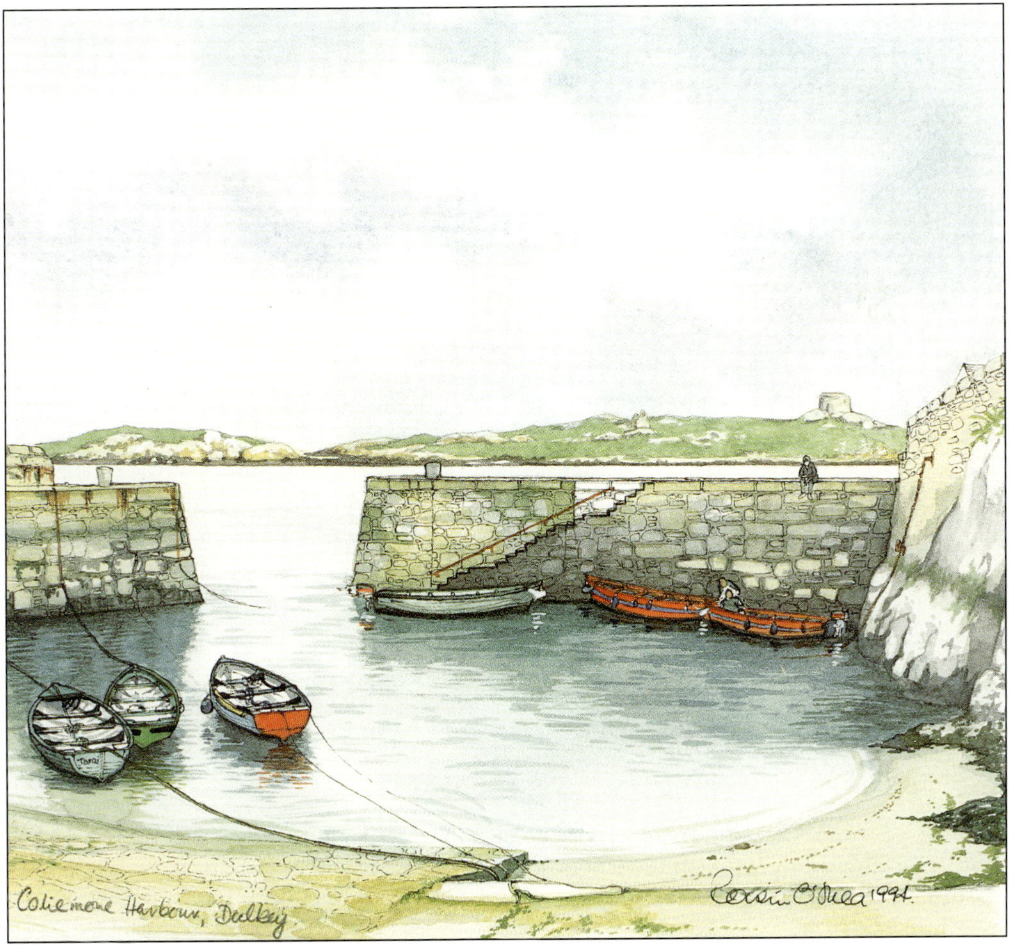
Coliemore Harbour, Dalkey

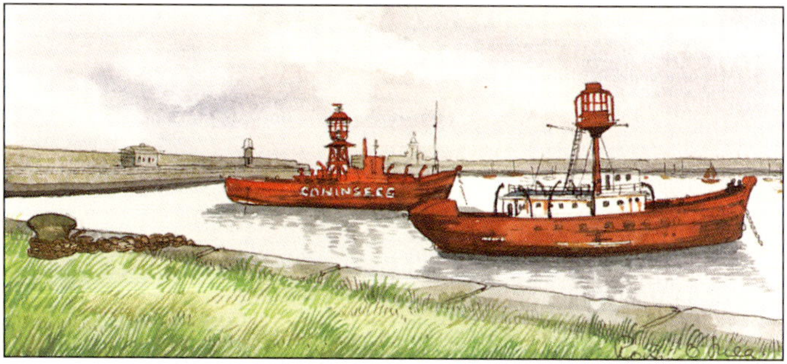

DUN LAOGHAIRE, DUBLIN

These kind of lightships have all but disappeared and are now replaced by automatic Landbys. The Kish was a lightship that had many accidents with other ships and was actually sunk by the Holyhead mailboat at one point. They were manned by a crew of seven who worked four weeks on and two weeks off in very trying conditions. One of these lightships is a floating maritime museum in Wexford and another of the ships in the painting is a floating clubhouse for the Sea Scouts. The Coninbeg lightship and the Tuskar Rock were guidelines by which to avoid the Saltee Islands. Dun Laoghaire has an excellent maritime museum.

BULLOCK HARBOUR, DUBLIN

In 1633 a Dutch ship was raided by pirates in the harbour, right in front of one of the royal ships that was berthed there. Security measures, as far as piracy was concerned, were very lax. During the summer months I like to sit in Bullock Harbour and soak in the sun, reading a good book, or swim a little in nearby Sandycove Harbour, where the traditional ice-cream van still sells ‘99’s’.

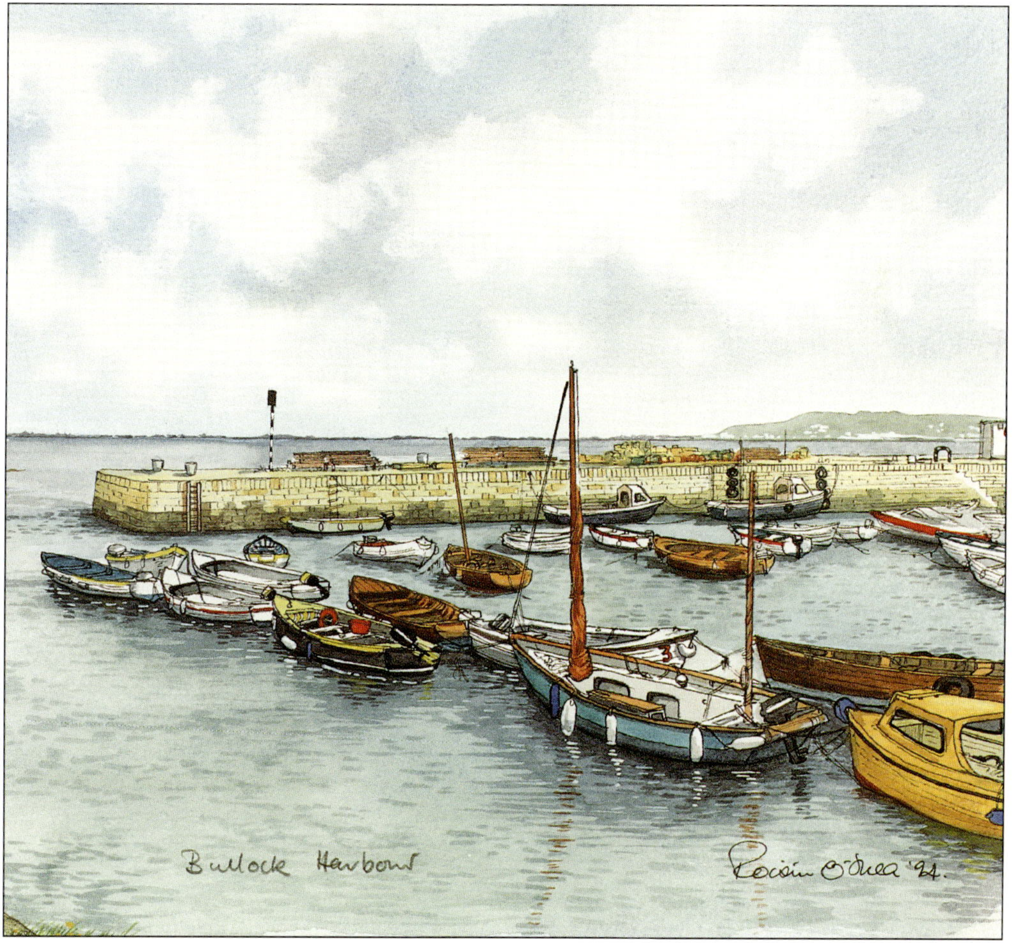
Bullock Harbour

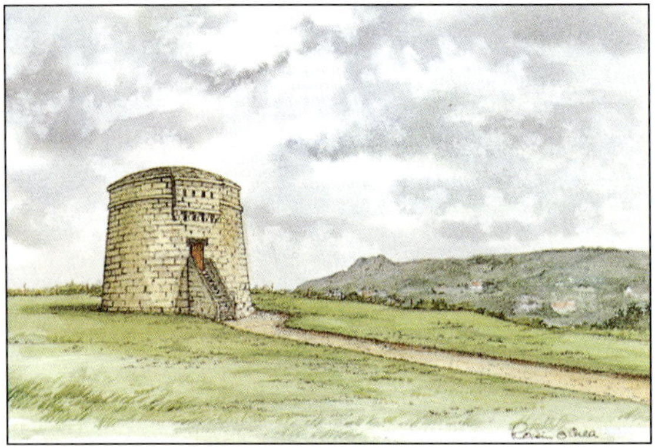

MARTELLO TOWER, HOWTH, DUBLIN

The Irish coastline is dotted with the famous Martello Towers, small round towers with flat roofs. These towers were designed and built as lookout posts during the Napoleonic Wars. Should an invading ship be spotted by one of the lookouts in the tower, he would make his way to the roof and set fire to a bundle of wood. This signal would eventually be seen by the next tower location, who in turn would do the same until all the towers along the coast would be notified of an approaching unidentified vessel. The Martello tower in this painting in Howth was transformed in the late 1800s to house the first trans-channel cable between England and Ireland.

POOLBEG TOWER, DUBLIN

Situated at the entrance to Dublin Bay.

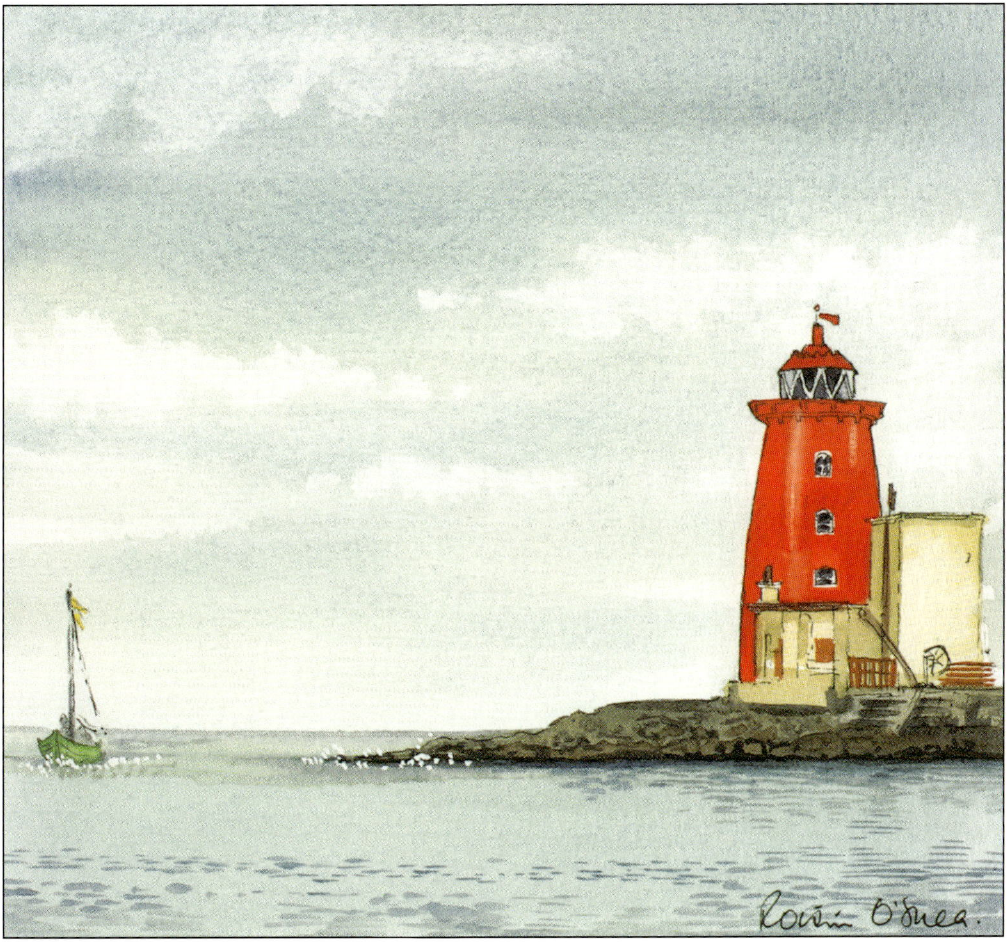
Roisin O'Shea.

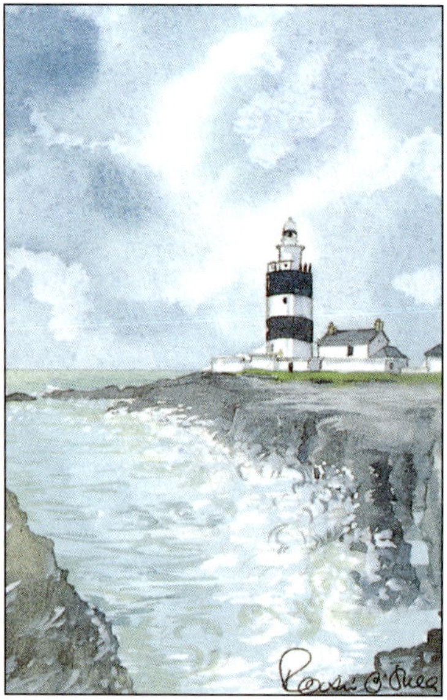

HOOK HEAD, WEXFORD

The famous expression "By Hook or by Crook" came from Oliver Cromwell when planning to attack Waterford in 1649. Hook referred to the Hook Peninsula, while Crooke is a small village just a short distance south from Passage East. The two places have thus achieved a place in history and lasting fame.

KILMORE QUAY, WEXFORD

This is a striking village with its lines of thatched cottages. On my travels around Ireland I have yet to see so many thatched cottages together and indeed, so many varieties. At the time that I did this painting this house was for sale; as an artist I couldn't picture a more fitting retreat during the summer months. An important deep-sea fishing centre is located here and the surrounding area is noted for good bass and pollock fishing.

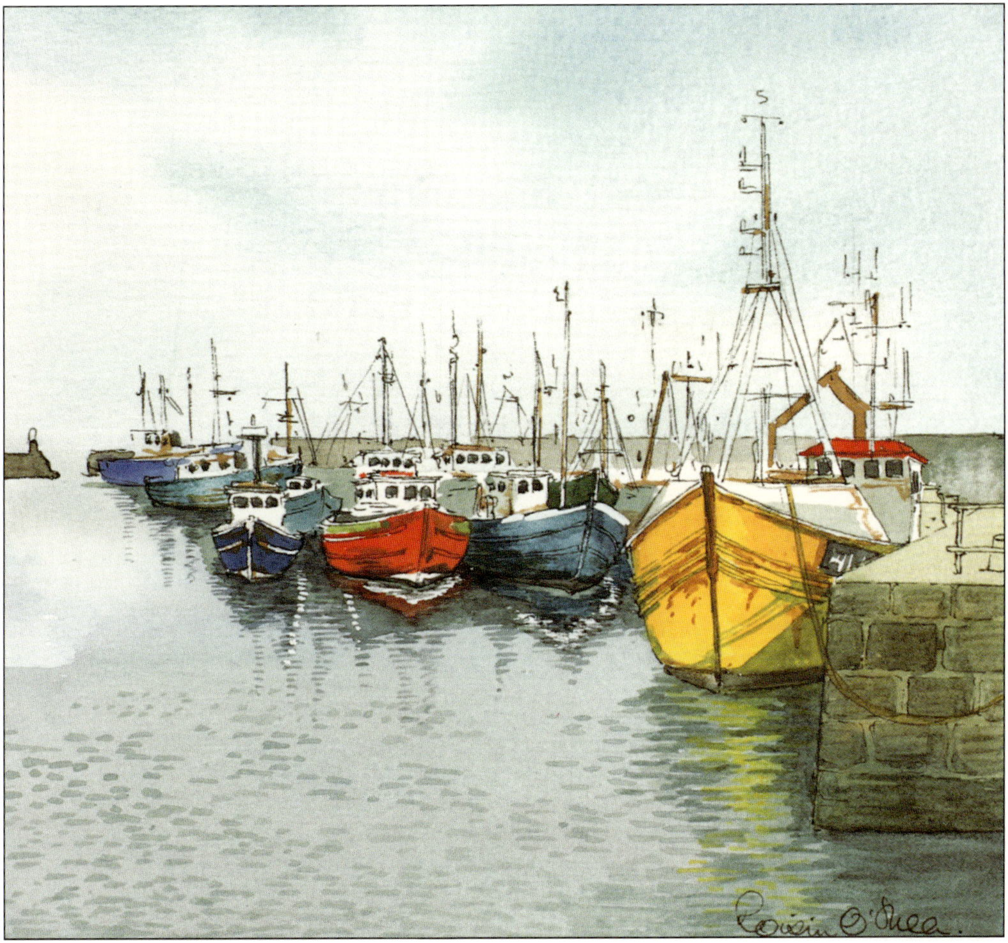

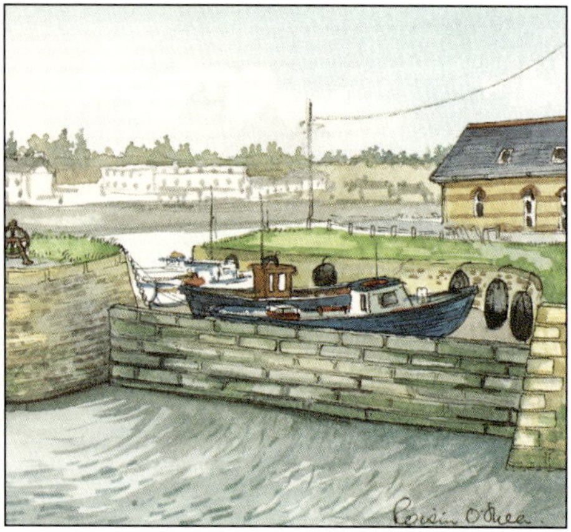

COURTOWN, WEXFORD

This harbour was built over one hundred and seventy years ago and is an exquisite village resort, peaceful and beautiful.

CARLINGFORD, LOUTH

This was once a fertile area of land between the Carlingford Mountains and the Mourne Mountains, or so legend would have it. It is said that a volcanic eruption caused the sea to flow over the area and in doing so drowned the prehistoric city of Cathar Linn, which means City of the Pool. It is also thought that the body of the legendary character Finn McCool lies in the hills behind Carlingford village. Carlingford is typical of a medieval village, though its rich history of course precedes this era. St. Patrick is thought to have landed here before venturing further to Strangford Lough, County Down, to begin his famous mission. The village was raided by the Vikings in the 8th and 9th centuries and again by the Normans in the 12th century.

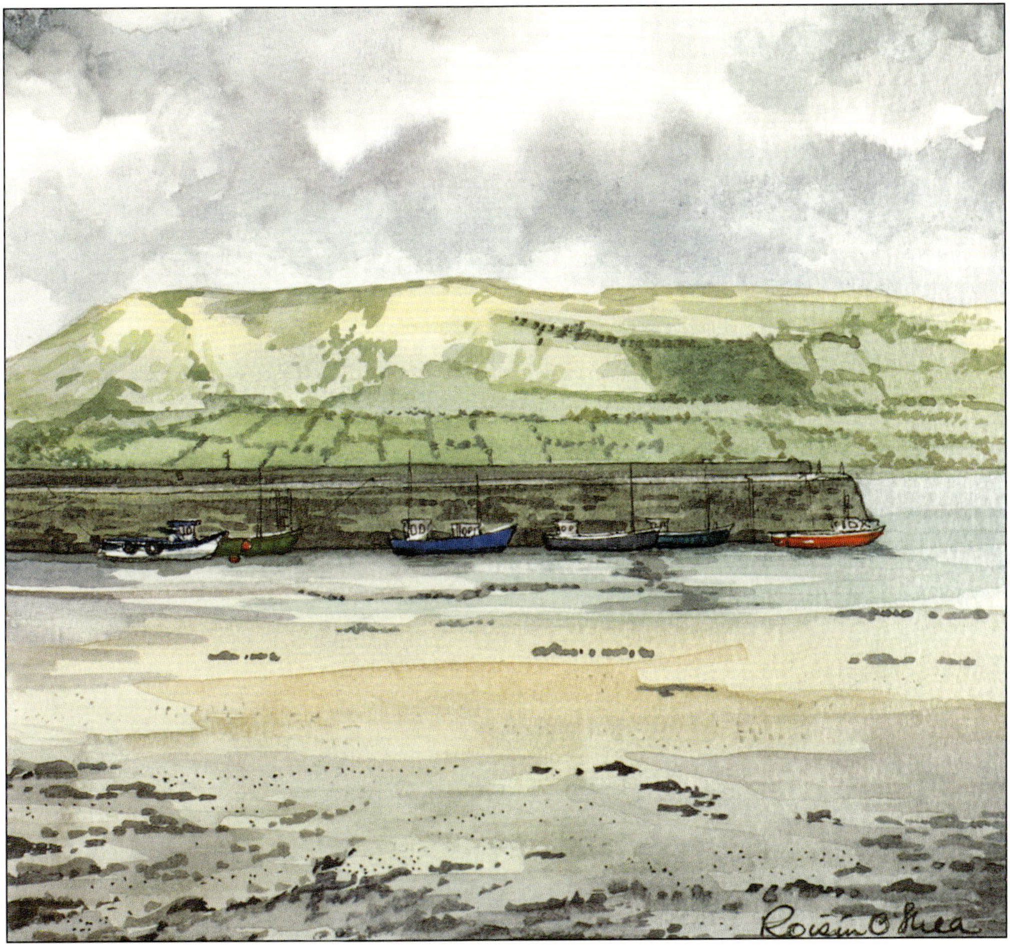
Roisin O'Shea

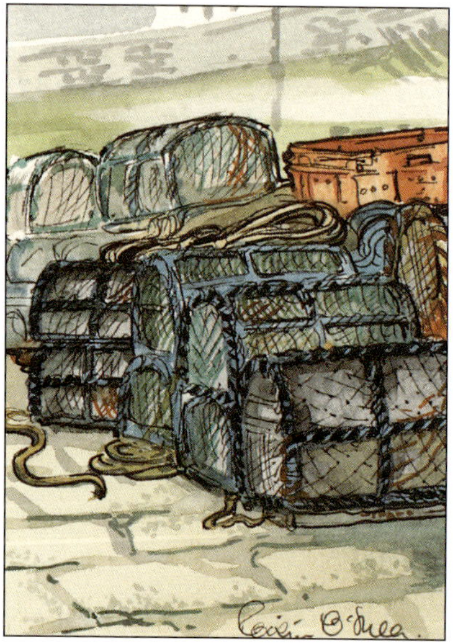

LOBSTER POTS

Putting down lobster pots is a popular livelihood in many parts of the country. The lobster that is usually caught and eaten is called the Common Lobster (Homarus gammarus). Its massive claws cut and crush food and protect it against predators such as seals. It feeds mainly at night on crabs, shellfish and other sea creatures, and grows periodically by shedding its skin. It is found in all coastal areas, mostly below the tide mark.

SKERRIES, DUBLIN

The name comes from the rock islands which lie off its coast, Red Island, Colt Island and Inis Patrick Island. It is said that St. Patrick crossed the harbour in low tide on his way to Ulster (hence the name Inis Patrick translates to St. Patrick Island). When I visited this harbour for my initial sketches, I locked my keys in the car and spent a relaxing two hours in the local bar listening to Garth Brooks while waiting for replacement keys – an unexpected pleasure.

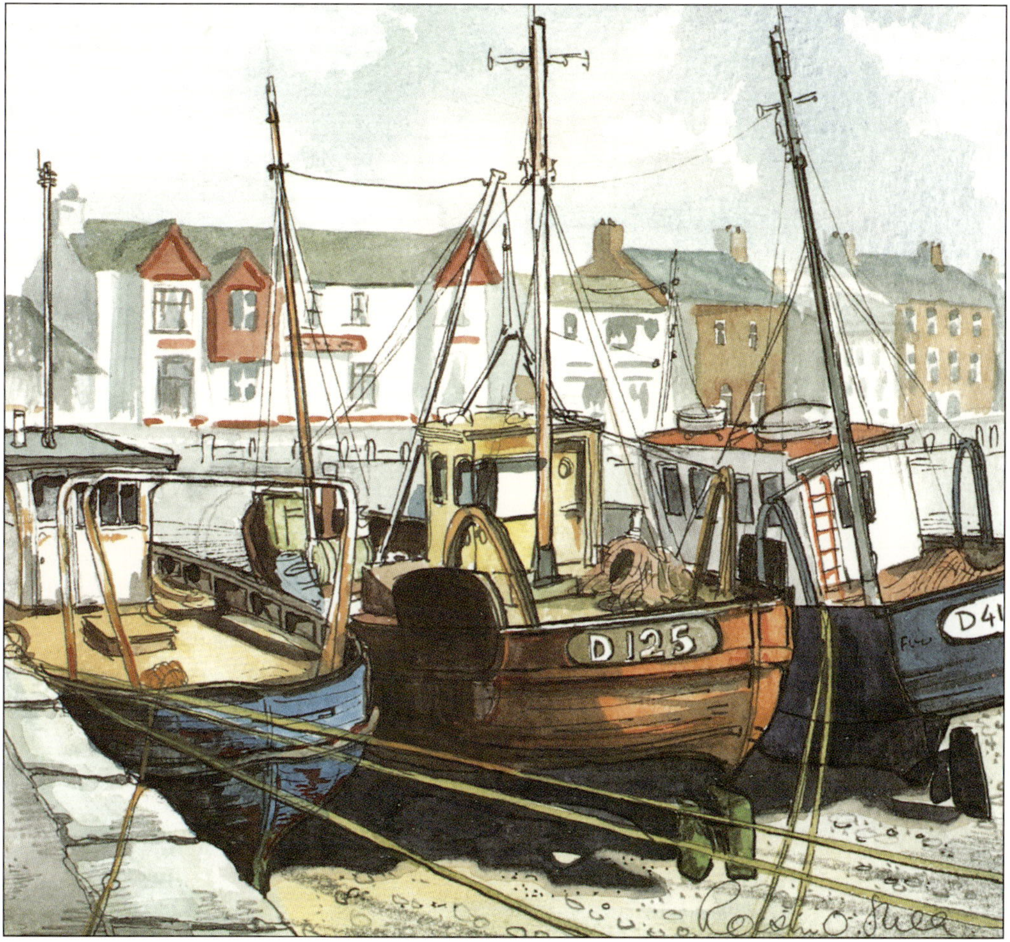
D125
D41

ROUNDSTONE, GALWAY

This town was created in the early 19th century when Alexander Nimmo, a Scotsman, settled here to do some maritime engineering work. He encouraged some Scottish fishermen to settle here also, and so a small English speaking community was set up in the midst of this Gaeltacht (Irish speaking) area. The original name was Cloch na Ron, cloch meaning stone; but ron means seal, not round, therefore it should have been Seal's Stone and not Roundstone. I spent many vacations in Roundstone in my late teens and early twenties – an abiding memory was my attempt to master rowing to the nearby island in a curragh.

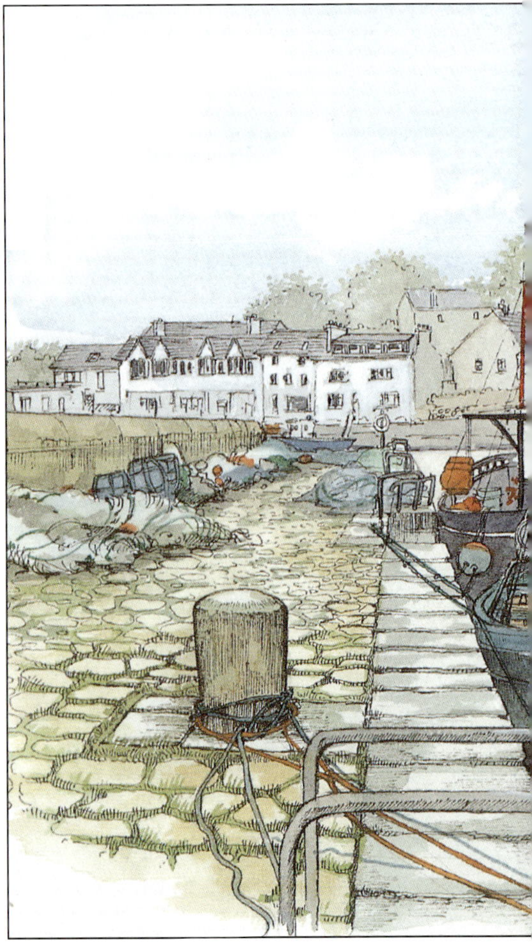

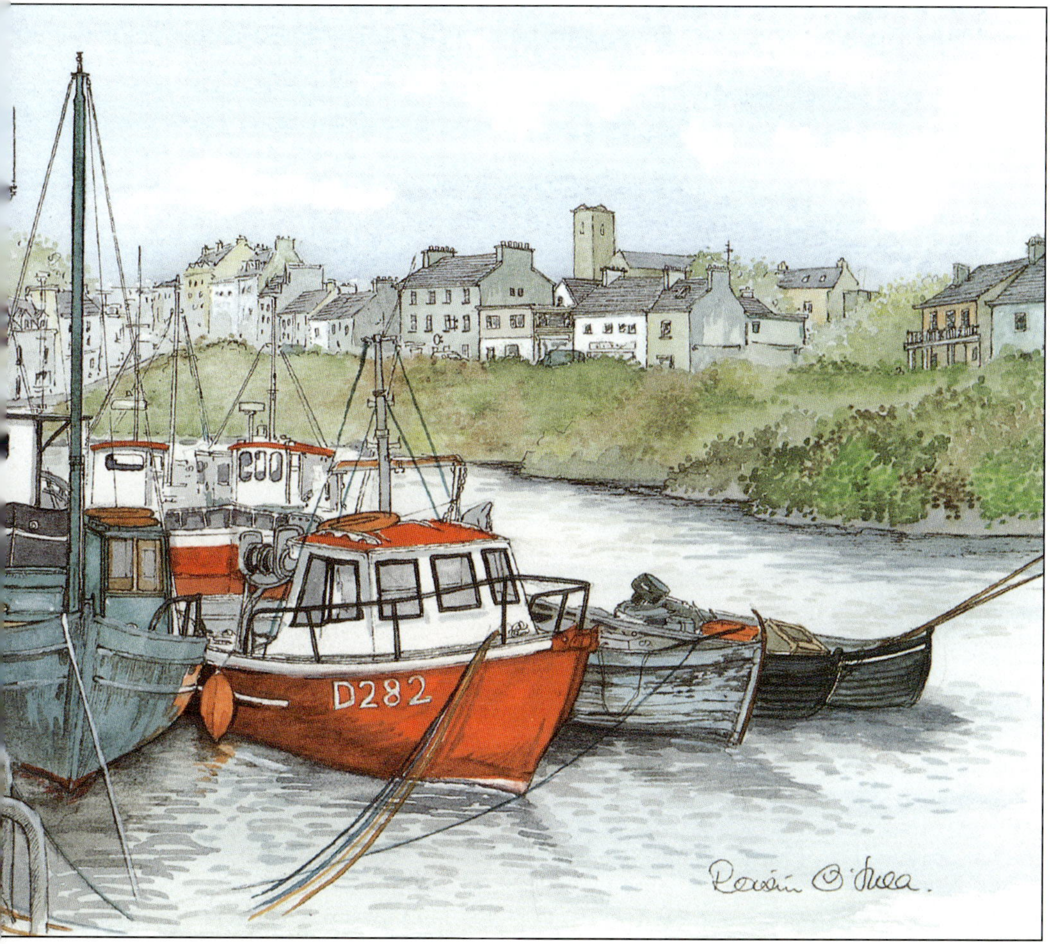
D282

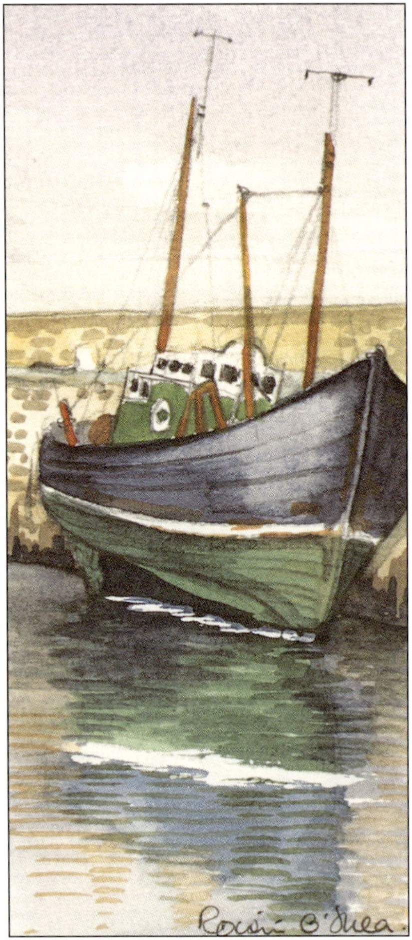

FISHING BOAT

Evidence of Irish shipbuilding is recorded as far back as the 6th century with St. Columba's crude wooden vessel. By the 13th century wooden rowed galleys were being built, followed by cogs in the 14th century which were replaced by the superior round-hulled vessels later that century. The shores of Antrim and Derry are considered to be the greatest sporting fishing areas, with many British and Irish records being achieved here. Among the range of fish to be found here are cod, bass, mackerel, whiting, plaice, haddock, spurdog and coalfish.

BOAT, ROUNDSTONE, GALWAY

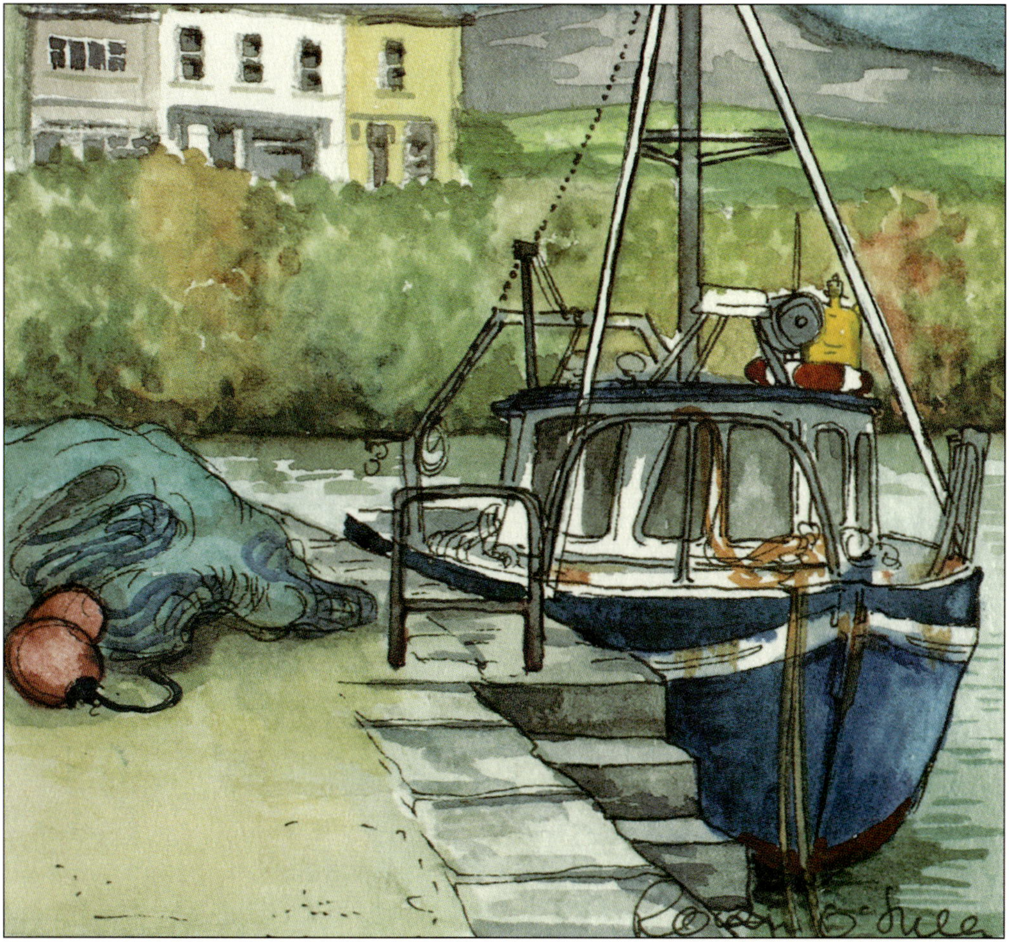

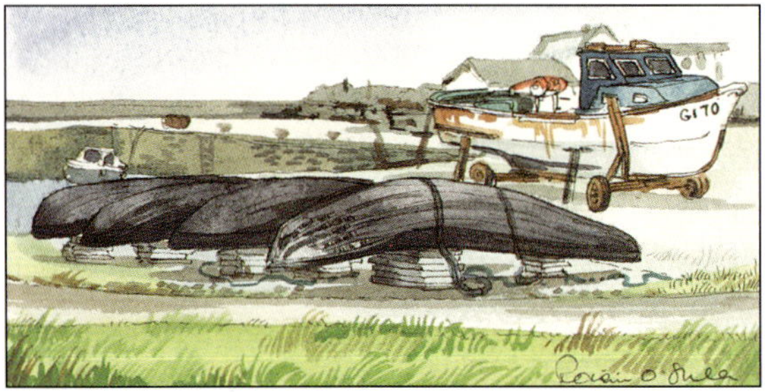

CURRAGHS, CLARE

Curraghs have been used for thousands of years and are still used today on the west coast and the Aran Islands. They have a light wooden frame made of drift-wood or bought timbers. The frame is covered with a tarred canvas stretched over the frame. On the Aran Islands old flour sacks were used, water-proofed with the tar. A curragh is black bellied and has a brown sail.

KINVARA, CLARE

Every year on the last Friday in August starts a three-day festival celebrating the hookers – 'Cruinniu na mBad' or the Gathering of the Boats. A fleet of these traditional boats races from Carraroe to the southern side of Galway Bay at Kinvara and are usually laden with turf. The submarine was invented by a Clare man, John Philip Holland, born in 1848. He submitted his designs to the U.S. Navy, who returned them as impractical. With money from a private source he finally launched a prototype in the Passaic River in 1878. It was capable of reaching twelve feet underwater and staying there for an hour. This machine is today on view in the Paterson Museum.

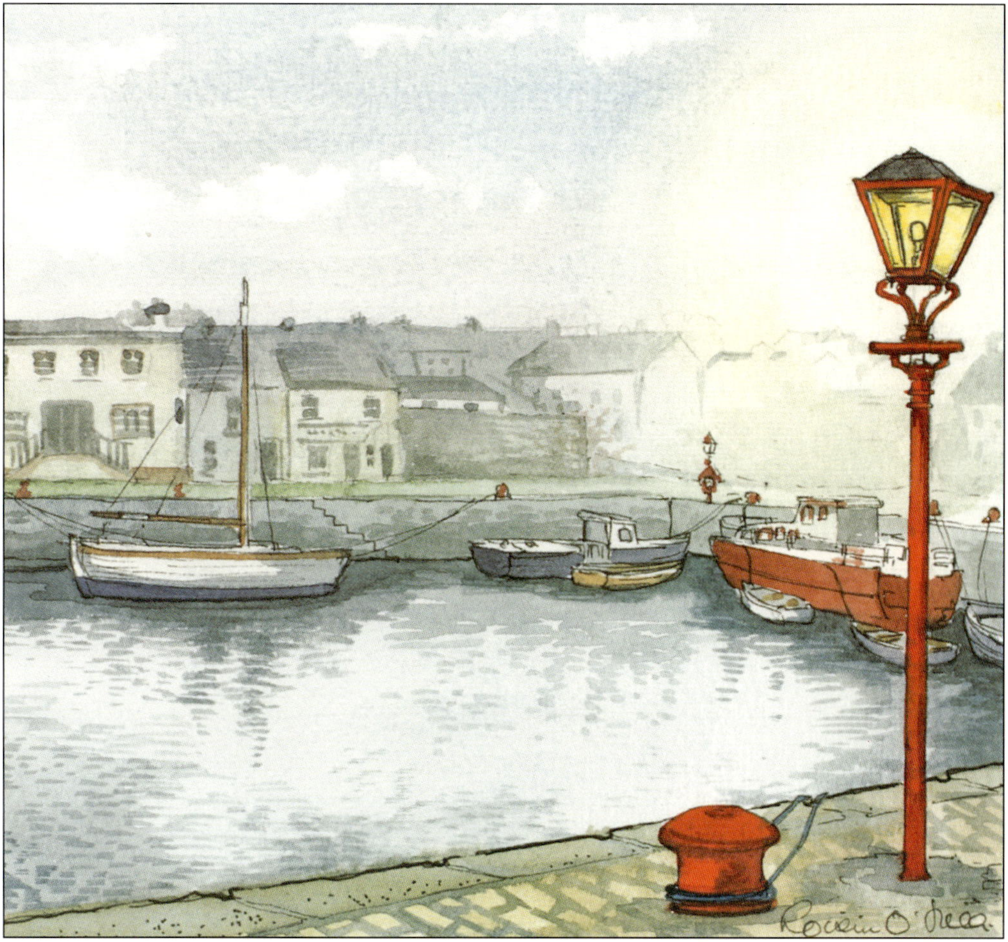

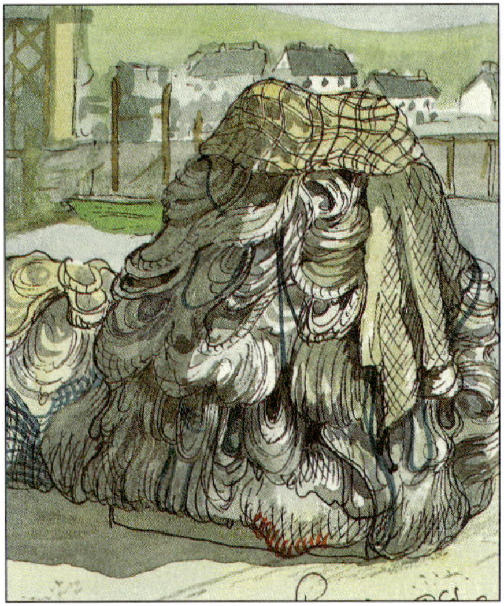

PILE OF NETS

There is an old seafaring tradition that seeing or even hearing about a fox, rabbit or hare meant that it would be bad luck to go out and fish that day. Mac Dara, the Celtic patron saint of fishermen, was supposed to have had the Christian name of Sionnach, meaning fox; it is for this reason that fishermen must show respect by dipping their sails three times on passing the island named after him. His feast day on July 16th is celebrated by a pilgrimage to his island by numerous vessels and a day of fun and races.

CARRIGAHOLT, CLARE

Situated near the estuary of the River Shannon, this fishing village's history dates back to the 1700s, when Donal O'Brien won the rights to the village after a battle with his renegade brother, the Earl of Thomond.

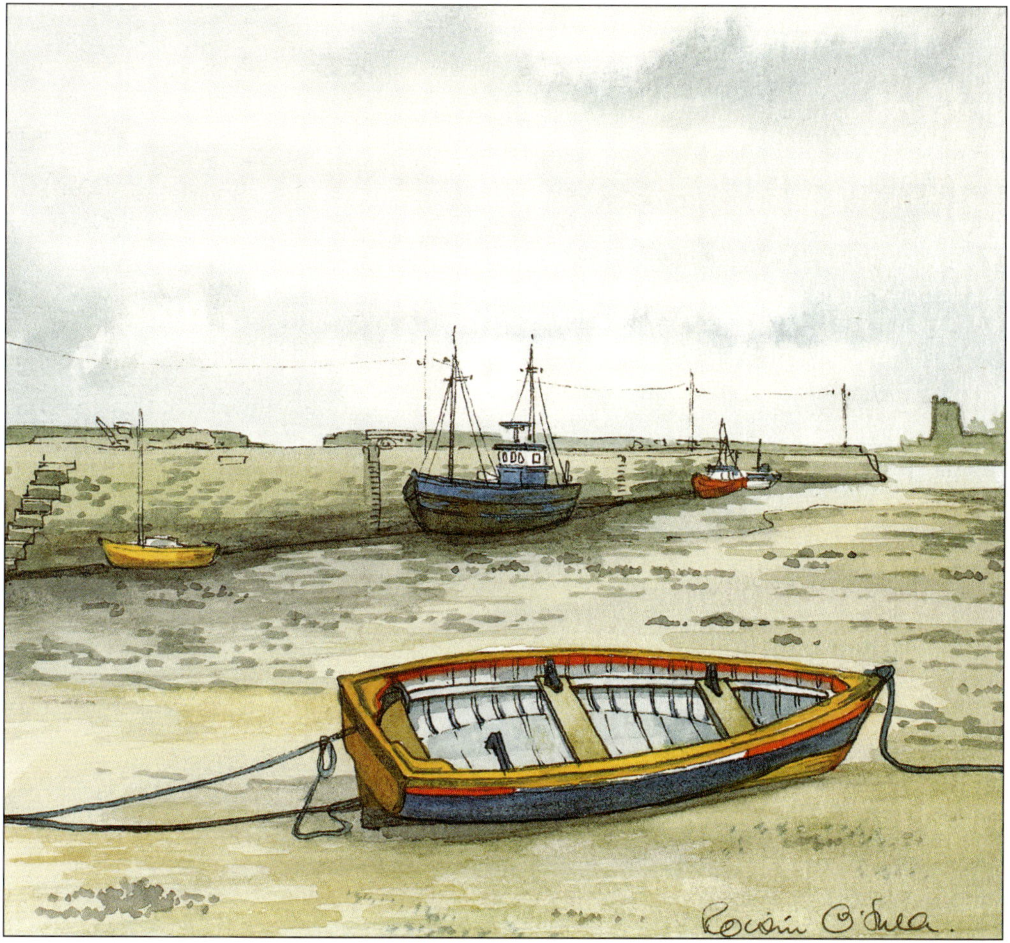
Roisin O'Shea.

MENDING NETS

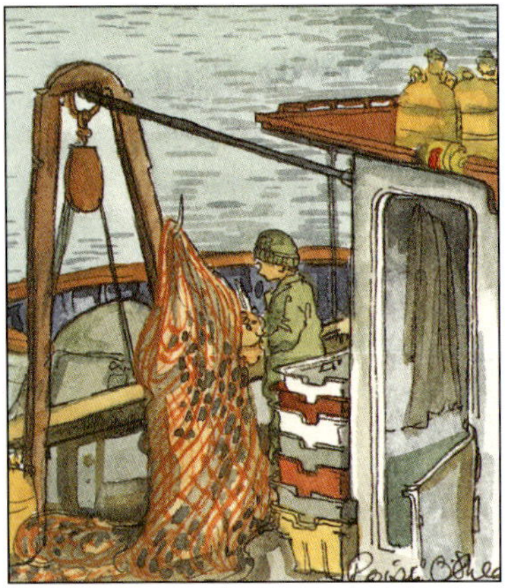

Herring are pelagic, surface-swimming, shoaling fish. Whiting are demersal, bottom-feeding, slow-moving solitary fish. Herring and mackerel are both migratory and arrive in our seas in large shoals. They feed and spawn here at regular intervals during the year. These fish were caught with drift nets which floated behind a boat and were suspended by floats. Fish were easily caught, as nets were let out at dusk and the darkness blinded the fish to their presence and they swam straight in.

CARRICKFERGUS, ANTRIM

Although more famous for its Norman Castle, built in 1180 by John de Courcy or Hugh de Lacy, Carrickfergus was the scene of the last witchcraft trial in Ireland. In 1711 eight women were found guilty of putting an evil spell on one Mary Dunbar, causing her to have fits. It was ascertained at a later date that these fits were caused by mildewed grain that was used for making-bread. This harbour is now one of the finest resort harbours in Ireland.

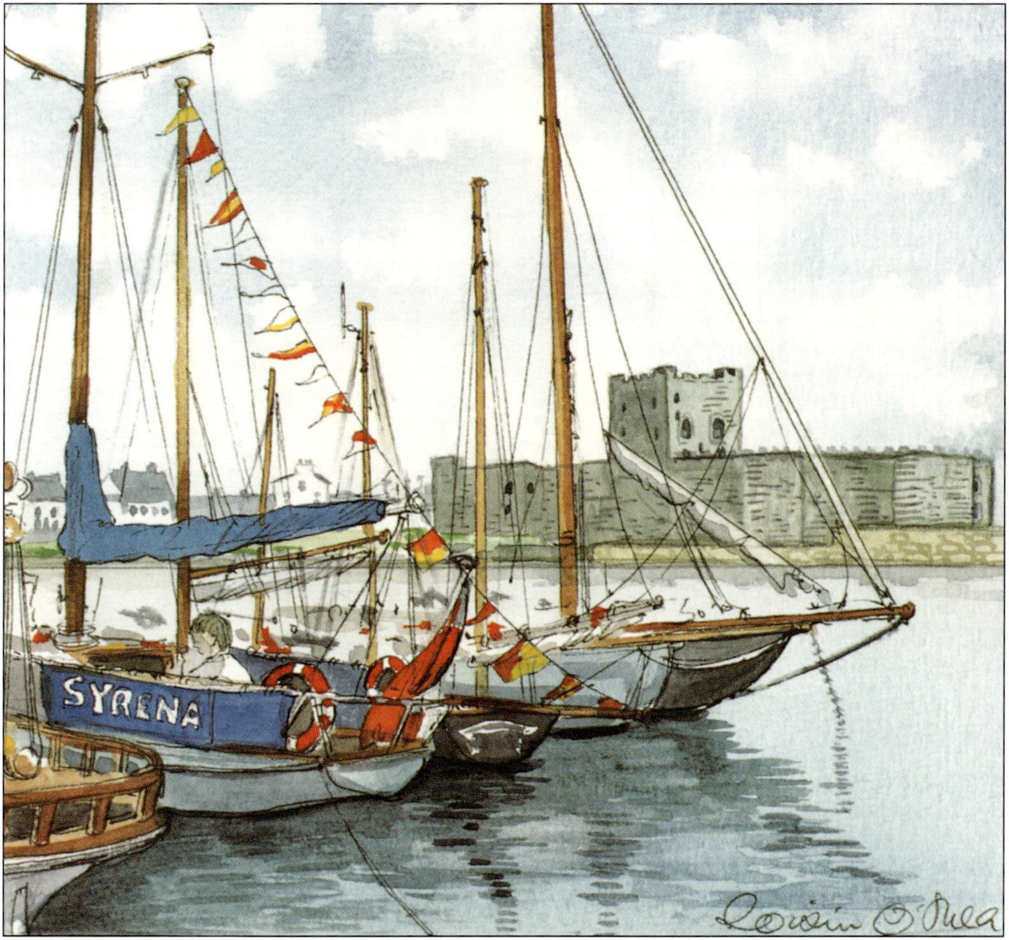
SYRENA
Roisin O'Shea

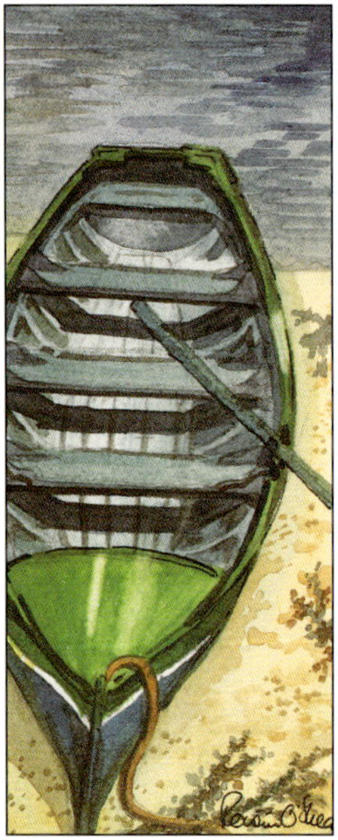

ROW BOAT

PORTBALLINTRAE, ANTRIM

A team of Belgian divers found an immense and very valuable store of Spanish Armada treasure between 1967 and 1968 off the Causeway coast. On the night of October 26th 1588, the galleon Girona was sunk in a severe storm, with only about five survivors out of 1,300 sailors. It was the largest of the Armada ships. Besides her own treasure, she also carried what had been salvaged from two other Spanish ships which had been wrecked previously. Amongst the 10,000 pieces of treasure included in the discovery were many beautiful, precious items of jewellery studded with rubies and pearls, and silver and gold coins. These items can be seen on display in the Ulster Museum, Belfast, County Antrim.

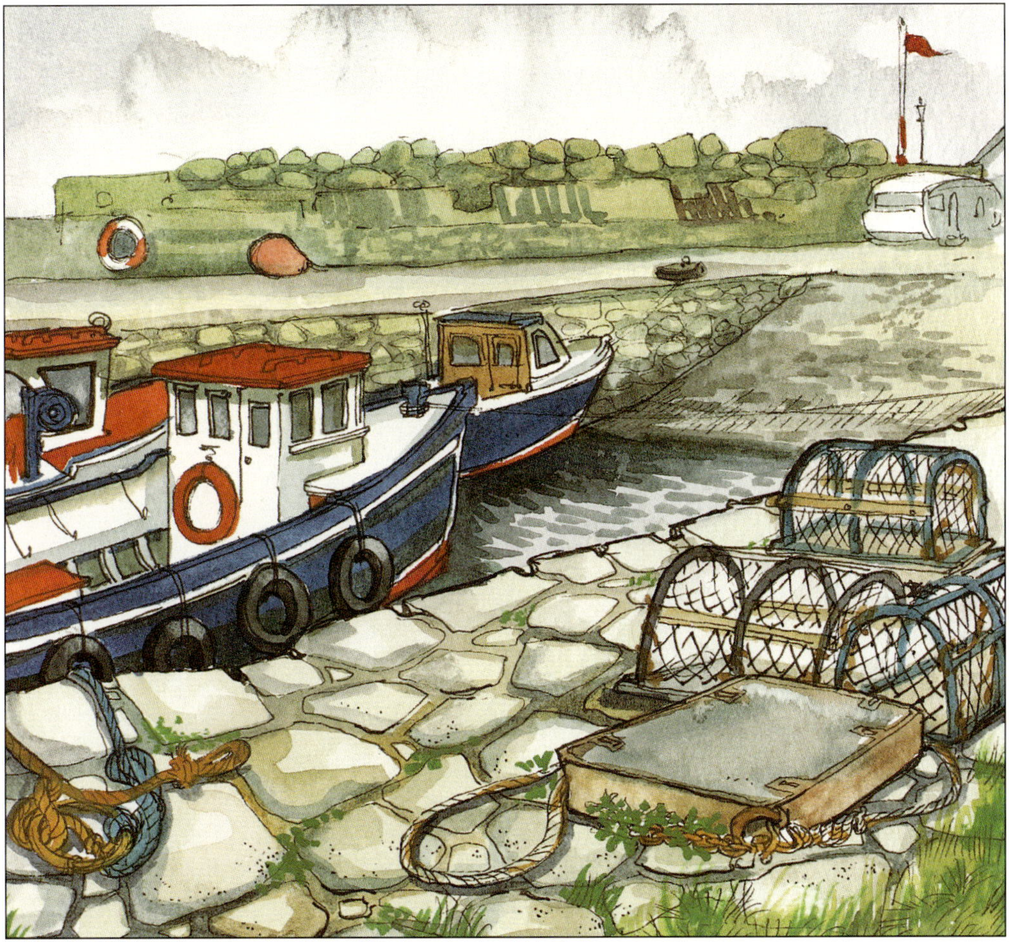

CUSHENDUN, ANTRIM

This village lies at the foot of Glendun, where the Glendun river meets the sea. It faces the North Channel and is only 28kms from Scotland. This village is now under the care of the National Trust. This beach-side hamlet is well-known for its row of beautiful Cornish-style cottages which were designed by Clough William-Ellis.
A hidden secret is the Cave House; it is only visible from the sea and is reached through a natural cave. Previously it was the home of John Masefield's wife, a Huguenot descendant. It is now a holiday home for nuns.

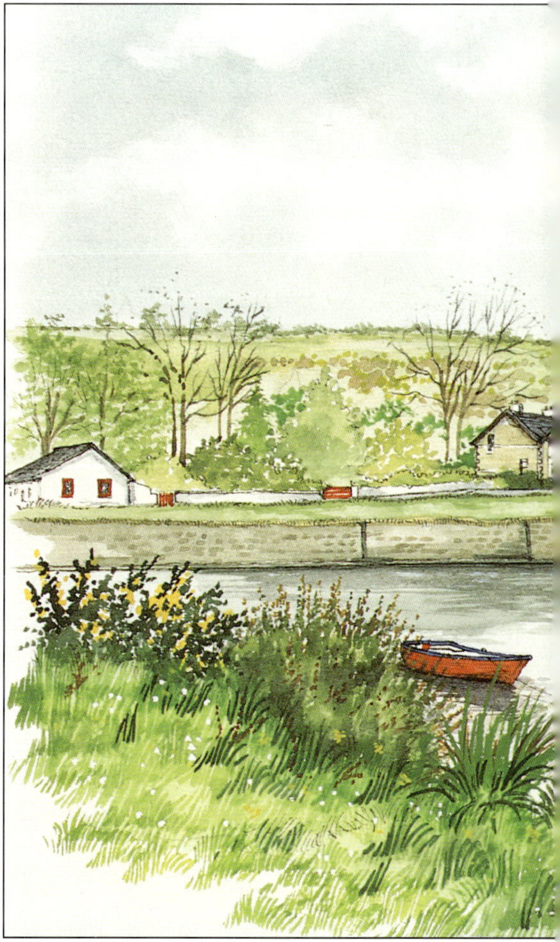

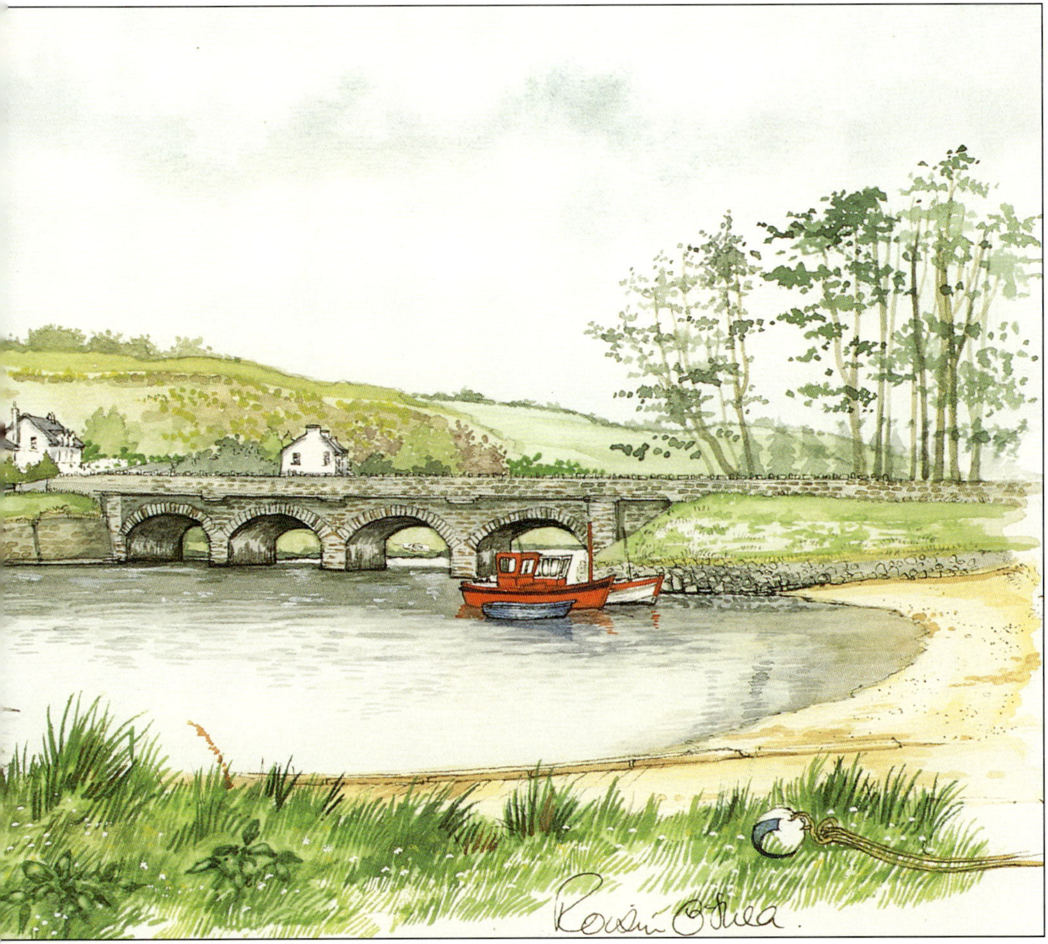
Roisin O'Shea

INDEX